M000118954

your little
red wagon

a conversation on approaching God

dr. alex himaya

Your Little Red Wagon
A Conversation on Approaching God
ISBN: 978-0-88144-429-2
Copyright © 2010 by Dr. Alex Himaya

Published by
Yorkshire Publishing Group
9731 East 54th Street
Tulsa, OK 74146
www.yorkshirepublishing.com

To those who have gone before...

My Parents! Leroy Faith, B.J. Rutledge, and the youth workers in the youth ministry at FBC Bossier in the '80s. The many pastors who have influenced me from afar and up close (and taught me the timeless principles and even illustrations found in this book).

Thanks for carrying the Good News of Jesus in such an attractive way that my generation could understand it and respond.

To those who are yet to come...

My faith family, The Church at BattleCreek, our friends in ministry and the believers who will carry the message of grace into the future and to the lives of those who Jesus died for!

Thanks for who you are and your faithfulness to the greatest message ever!

I love you!

contents

foreword

There's something almost magical about an old Radio Flyer wagon, isn't there?

It conjures up all kinds of images and memories. Even Hollywood knows the nostaligic value of a little red wagon. The sight of one stirs my emotions and takes me back to my childhood. You may or may not have had a wagon, but you at least knew someone who did. For boys, it was for hauling rocks, dirt, and resources to the fort (usually stuff we compiled from friends' garages or trash). For girls, it was a

magical carriage used to carry the most
beautiful of all princesses. Or, as for my
daughter, it was a mobile pet store filled
with stuffed animals for sale. The beauty of
the wagon is in its ambiguity.

It can be whatever we imagine.

I have another little red wagon, and so
do you. An imaginary one. You and I
started piling stuff into these imaginary
wagons so early in life that we can hardly
remember the first things that went into
them. But if somehow we could turn back
time, we would see that as children everything we loaded into our wagons was posi-
tive. Great memories. New discoveries. It
stored a world of wonder for an imagina-
tive, curious, innocent little mind.

But somewhere along the way, we
discovered tragedy, pain, disappointment,
and disillusionment. Those too went into

the wagon. And we felt the sting. Our once weightless, lighthearted wagons turned into dump trucks, and we started to feel the weight.

As time passes, our piles grow higher and higher—lots of it great, but much of it bad. We attempt to bury the bad underneath all the good stuff so that no one else can see it. And so we're content and comfortable as long as no one begins to dig through our wagon to see who we really are. Because who wants to deal with me and all my issues? Not me. Not you. Certainly not God, right?

Wrong.

What if there is someone who cares about absolutely everything we have in our wagons? Good or bad.

Beautiful or shameful. And is unshaken by any of it? What if we could let go of the wagon, drop the handle and not worry about it anymore? No more shame. No more lies. No more hiding. What if you no longer had to worry about the good sutff covering the bad stuff because neither matters?

If you're looking, like I was, for that kind of freedom, read on. Breathe deep. Exhale. Let go. Watch your wagon go "flying" and enjoy the release. I want you to know that the freedom you've been seeking can be found in these pages.

Proceed *without* caution.

chapter 1

your little red wagon

It was Africa-hot that summer in Louisiana where I grew up. The water level in the bayou, a couple of blocks up the street from my house, was receding like an old man's hairline. The banks were drying and cracking. That afternoon my brother, Paul, and our friend, Jeff, and I were playing as usual on the old man's bridge. From that vantage point above the receding water, we saw what looked like a snake slithering through the murky water below.

Even though we were only nine and ten years old, we had killed probably a dozen or more snakes in our short lifetimes. If reality TV was around then, we could have had our own show...*The Snake Hunters*.

On a closer look, we realized that this creature was some sort of eel or large fish. Knowing that the younger kids would be playing on down the bayou, we believed it was our sovereign duty to rid the waters of any danger. We felt compelled to make the waters safe again. That day we had failed to bring our Daisy Red Rider and Crossman air rifles, which were standard issue for all the neighborhood boys in Bossier City. The only weapon we brought along that day was my friend Jeff's Louisville Slugger. Drawing straws left me as the one responsible for engaging the beast and protecting the waters.

So I grabbed the slugger and made it live up to its name. I waded into the water and beat the living daylights out of the intruder. Mud, moss, and millions of bacteria filled my mouth, nose, and other orifices. After a long-fought battle, the wounded foe floated to the top of the water in defeat. When I picked it up to hold over my head victoriously, I saw that its mouth was filled with razor-sharp teeth. The "hebee gebees" ran up and down my spine at the thought that I could have been bitten. That day we were introduced to alligator gar.

Suddenly, Paul yelled, "Alex, look out behind you!" I splashed and flailed my way out of the muddy bayou faster than a speeding bullet (no wait, that was superman, but I was moving!). Turning to look, I saw what seemed like dozens of alligator gar coming to their friend's rescue. So what did I do? I called for back-up too! My buddies and I ran home to get a couple more bats and to put on our pea-green rubber boots. We meant business.

That afternoon Paul, Jeff and I waged war and took no hostages. We slaughtered every single alligator gar fish in our bayou. The sheriff (Brodey, I think?) from *Jaws* would have been proud. Realizing that there were enough fish on the shore to feed a small army, we headed home to get something to help us transport our war trophies. We filled two large black Hefty trash bags with fish and worked together to load them into our RadioFlyer red wagon.

On the journey home, Jeff said, "We can feed the entire neighborhood! We are heroes!" We thought that if Jesus could feed thousands with a few fish, we were about to be a part of the miracle on the bayou.

We thought that if Jesus could feed thousands with a few fish, we were about to be a part of the miracle on the bayou.

As we arrived back home, Paul rang the doorbell at our house, signaling for mom to come witness our triumphant return. I will never forget the look on my mom's face. It was the same look she made when our puppy pooped on the floor—sheer disgust! Here we were as nine- and ten-year-old boys as proud as could be with our catch. We believed we had not only scored the deadliest catch, but also that we could provide a fish fry for the entire neighborhood. Normally, my mother was my biggest fan. She proudly displayed my watercolor family portrait (looking past the humpty-dumpty bodies with sticks for arms and legs) for all the world to see. She cheered me on when I raced bikes (even the year I got the crash award). But at that moment, the one person on the planet who was proud of me when I struck out in t-ball was horrified with our catch. We really knew we were in trouble when she yelled for my dad, "Mack," and his name lengthened to seven syllables. We were so confused. Why was she so upset?

I learned a lesson that day that still impacts my relationship with God. The issue was perspective. My mom and I both had strong opinions, or perspectives, about what was in that wagon, but they were very different!

We all have a wagon that we've filled with a lifetime of works and deeds, both good and bad. And we have a tendency to believe that what's in the wagon affects our relationship with God. You might view what's in your wagon like I viewed mine— with great pride, OR you might see it like my mom saw it with great disgust. Your perspective on how you believe God views what's in your wagon, will determine how you approach God or if you approach Him at all.

chapter 1 questions:

Have you ever shared a personal accomplishment with someone and felt disappointed by their response?

Why was their perspective different from yours?

How does the principle of *perspective* impact our point of view?

What could you do, or not do, to influence God's view of you?

chapter 2

stinkin' fish or golden nuggets? depends on perspective

Since that day on the bayou, my perspective on almost everything has changed. Now that I have three kids of my own, I am continually wishing they could see things from my perspective. For example, if my kids could see friendship, health, or education from my perspective, it certainly would make their young lives much easier. Knowing what I know now, I would have worried less about what my friends thought about me and more about learning something in school. While our perspectives on many things hopefully mature as we get older, it seems that our perspective of what is in our wagon remains random and problematic.

So, what's in your wagon? First, let me tell you that the problem with our little red wagons is that each of us has our own perspective or opinion on what's good and what's bad. Because of my perspective (or collection of life circumstances), I have a list of things that fall into different categories:

- ❏ things that really tick God off
- ❏ things that kinda tick Him off
- ❏ things that He doesn't really like
- ❏ those things that are probably bad, but "hey, nobody's perfect"

19

The problem, again, is perspective. None of our lists are exactly the same.

We allow our whole approach to God to be governed by a personal list of do's and don't that WE prioritize as WE see fit. We all make them up because there is no such list in the Bible, categorizing big sins and little sins. It's also hard to find common ground on our lists, except with the really big stuff and the really trivial things. For example, you might agree with me that speeding doesn't bother God that much as long as nobody gets hurt. So from our perspective, that's not a big deal. Nobody's going to lose sleep thinking, *I am going to hell for speeding.* (If you are...put down this book and make an appointment with a counselor immediately.) Murder? We all agree that's a really bad one. (If you don't, then turn yourself in.) But what if you're holding this book right now, and you are involved in a sin that moral America would view as a "biggie"? You might feel that your relationship with God is pretty good. He loves you, and He understands your sin because He knows what's going on in your life. Because of your life circumstances or perspective, this one might not make your "really bad" list any more.

What about lying? Some lies are worse than others—aren't they? What about a mental sin like lust? What about just imagining what you'd like to see happen to your enemies? How wrong is that? If we compare our lists, these sins will fall into a wide variety of categories because they are being sorted by a wide variety of judges.

The way we view the contents of our wagon is relative to what we are comparing them to. If we know a guy at work is cheating on his wife, what's in our wagon might look good. If someone else's child is expelled from school for fighting or cheating, we wipe our foreheads and think, *Hey, I'm okay. My kid is still enrolled!* As long as we're keeping track of other people's challenges and what they have in their wagons, our own wagon looks better. Again, it comes back to perspective.

But, you might be of a less optimistic mindset. Your neighbor's child is always polite when you see him, and your child is beating the neighbor's cat, so the "bad" in your wagon feels heavier. You read a book about happy marriages, and yours doesn't seem to match up. So, throw another "stinky fish" on the wagon.

In truth we probably alternate between these two views depending on where we are emotionally at any given time. The point is that how we view the stuff in our wagons (good or bad) is so random. It's relative to what we've done lately and to whose wagon we are comparing ours. Could it be that God is much more concerned with "us" than with what is in our wagons?

> Could it be that God is much more concerned with "us" than with what is in our wagons?

chapter 2 questions:

What would you put on a list of "really bad" sins?

Describe a time when you felt really good about the contents of your wagon because of whose you were comparing to at the moment.

Describe a time when you felt really bad about the contents of your wagon because of whose you were comparing it to.

chapter 3

the wagon and the wall

In my story from my perspective, my mom was ticked and disgusted with me. In my mind, a wall had gone up between us. She was on one side of the fish, and I was on the other. From her perspective she was just plain disgusted. She was going to gladly give the wagon filled with fish to my friend, Jeff, take me inside, put me in the bath, brush my teeth, read me a bedtime story, and put me to bed. While the wagon load of fish was a problem, it was not an unsurpassable obstacle for my mother. I thought my adventures in the bayou were about to be over for good, and she just thought I was stinky and needed a bath. Often times we let our assumptions and perspective overtake a situation.

In your relationship with other people, you've seen what happens when you offend, mistreat, cheat, or sin against someone else. You've seen an emotional wall go up between the person you hurt and yourself. If you're married, you see this from time to time, even when you are deeply in love. You do the wrong thing or unintentionally say something offensive, and you can sense a shift taking place between the two of you, even when your spouse doesn't say a word.

Our first Christmas as a married couple, Meredith dropped hints that she wanted a locket on a necklace. Ten minutes after she gave me that clue, my mother called and asked for help in picking out a Christmas gift for Meredith. I told my mom to get her a locket and chain. I was covered; I had already ordered all of Meredith's gifts from catalogues and had them shipped to my mom and dad's house. We drove from seminary housing in Fort Worth, Texas, to my parent's house in Louisiana a couple of days before Christmas. On Christmas Eve, NONE of the items I ordered had arrived so I had NO gift for my wife on our first Christmas together. In a panic I talked my mom into letting me have the locket to give to Meredith and convinced her to go get something else.

Christmas morning was wonderful! Meredith's reaction to the fact that I had gone and picked out the sweetest, most perfect locket for her was priceless—there were even tears! She was so touched by my thoughtfulness. Later that night she said, "One day, if we have a daughter, I will give it to her and tell her 'Your daddy gave me this on our first Christmas.'" I know Christmas is all about Jesus, but I certainly felt like the hero of that Christmas. Over the next couple of days, questions like, "Where and when did you get it?" led to a series of white lies. Eventually, the 'lie train' crashed and what was an amazing first Christmas gift blew up in my face like a nuclear bomb. The reality that I had spent no time or effort picking out the locket stripped it of its emotional value for Meredith, and in that moment, I felt the great wall of China rise up between us. Instead of it becoming a treasured family heirloom, the story has become a lesson for my sons, and all males, to follow. Meredith eventually forgave me, but even now 15 years later, some Christmases the story of the locket finds its way back.

If you're a parent, you've seen it with your children. I can see in the eyes of my children when a wall goes up because I've offended them, been insensitive, or not listened to them. In a moment of frustration or excitement if I raise my voice, I can see the wall that rises up between us. Several years ago our community group at church volunteered at a local women's shelter. Meredith and I took all three kids with us. This led to some lengthy conversations with our five year-old daughter, Katherine, about who would live in a shelter and why. A few days later, in a moment of frustration and impatience, I yelled at the kids. At bedtime that night, Katherine informed me that when I raise my voice it makes her want to go live in a women's shelter. At a very young age, she sensed the wall that had gone up between us emotionally.

Whenever an emotional wall goes up, we know that it can take some time for the wall to come down, depending on the nature of the offense. If it's a small offense, it might take an hour. If it's a bigger offense, it might be a day. In some cases it can be weeks, months, even years. It would seem to make perfect sense to take this whole system and think that this must be how a relationship with God works—but it's not.

From our perspective, we assume that God throws up a wall between Himself and us when we sin. After all, He's holy— and must be wholly incapable of hanging out with sinners. That's why ever since the Garden of Eden, He has been "out there somewhere" beyond our ability to walk with Him. In our minds God is like the wind; we know He's there, but we can't see Him. Sometimes we view Him as a gentle breeze, and other times, like a raging tornado coming after us and the contents of our wagon.

In our minds because of what is in our wagons, we don't measure up. We don't imagine God with a wagon trailing Him, so we think *Why would God want to deal with me and my wagon full?* And we just assume that our emotions accurately reflect His feelings toward us! In life, never assume. When you assume, and then don't attempt to try things because you think you know how they'll play out, you miss out altogether.

Often we think, *If I could just be good enough* or *if I could get my act together—then somehow my standing will go up in God's eyes.*

God doesn't care about what you're carrying around, and He's not into building walls either. He is much more interested in having an intimate relationship with you.

We believe that if we can make ourselves a little more consistent, a little more lovable, and a little closer to God, we'll end up more acceptable to Him. But the truth is, God doesn't care about what you're carrying around, and He's not into building walls either. He is much more interested in having an intimate relationship with you.

chapter 3 questions:

Have you ever told a "little white lie" only to have it turn into a major mistake? When did you feel like you had crossed the proverbial "line"?

What stands out in your life right now that if you could just fix it, or remove it from your life, would improve your standing before God?

What is an assumption that you have made in your life about God?

chapter 4

the prodigal

There's a story in the Bible that's not too different from mine. It's a story of a son who had been gone for awhile, and while he was out, he had filled his wagon with a bunch of filthy, rotten junk.

It's a story about a father and his two sons...two sons whom he loved very much. Each son received an inheritance. The older brother chose to stay close and made his father very proud. The younger brother...not so much. He ran off to sow his wild oats, squandered his inheritance until he had nothing left and was forced to return home. You may have heard of this story. It's commonly called the story of The Prodigal Son.

We'll pick up this story as the younger brother (bad boy) is making his way home. Let's imagine for a moment that he, too, had a little red wagon that he towed around (maybe back then it was Red Sea Flyer) a wagon now cluttered full of junk from his misadventures. It's important to remember that this bad boy had an older brother. A perfect, never-did-anything-wrong, make-you-sick-he's-so-good kind of brother. His brother, "good boy," had been at home working, eating, talking, laughing, bonding with his dad the whole time, "bad boy" was out doing…well…"bad boy" things. We've all been or played the role of the "bad boy" before, so put yourself there now.

Imagine the thoughts he must have been having as he got closer to the house. We've all had moments like this. Think back when you were a teen—you stayed out too late and just knew that your parents were steaming behind the door. "Bad boy" knew that his father wouldn't approve of his boy-gone-wild adventure, worse yet, the junk he had collected in his wagon. It was filthy. *How will we ever be reconciled?* He thought. As he walked anxiously, he was analyzing the contents of his wagon. Debating on whether to leave it as is, deal with the consequences, and hope that his father loved him enough to accept him anyway. Or, maybe he should empty it real quick of the bad stuff before he gets home? Leaving only what he wanted his father to see.

He stops and looks at the wagon, then the house that's now within sight. Then he stares at the wagon again. His heart is racing with anxiety and anticipation. What's father going to think? Will he still love me? Will he forgive me? Have I disappointed him so much that he's disowned me?

Stop here for a moment. I want you to think of the very best father you've ever known. Maybe it's your father. Maybe it's not. Maybe yours is the worst father you've ever known, but you've seen others and wished your father was like them. Imagine that guy now and all the wonderful qualities he possesses.

A good father is strong but gentle. Loving but firm. Generous. Trustworthy. Forgiving. Our father in this story was all of that and more. So imagine what he must have been thinking on this glorious day.

His boy was coming home. Finally, he could hug him again, tell him how much he loved him and missed him. He could laugh with him over meals. He could share his experiences and wisdom with him as they worked together. He could once again be all the things that a loving father is to his son.

As he sees his long lost son come over the horizon, now just minutes away, his heart was racing with anticipation. Overflowing with love and joy, he ran to meet him. He was thinking only of the embrace that they were about to have and how he would tell him over and over, I forgive you. I love you. I've missed you.

I forgive you. I love you. I've missed you.

You're finally home where you belong. We will throw a huge party!

See, it's all about perspectives…. The boy's perspective and the dad's perspective on the situation were very different.

Just like our heavenly Father, the father in this story didn't see a wagon or any of his son's baggage. All he saw was, simply, his son. And that was all that mattered. His son was returning home.

chapter 4 questions:

Do you have any "if only I..." regrets in your life? How are they impacting you today?

What would you be willing to do to be forgiven by someone you've hurt in your life?

reconciling more than your locks

What happened between the father and the son is called reconciliation.

The word *reconciled* is monumental. It means "to be made compatible." Recently we changed all the hardware, including some of the exterior doorknobs and dead-bolts in our house. I guess it was time for us to exit the greatest decade ever, the '80s. For the first time in most of our married lives, the opportunity to have one key work in every lock was one of the benefits. The process of making this a reality was a lesson for me. I had never understood what locksmiths actually do. We had to take the key from one of the locks we were not replacing to the locksmith. He then made all of the new locks fit that key. The process was fascinating. On the inside of each lock are many series of pins that can be in what seemed like an endless array of positions each. This process is reconciliation. Two things that were at odds with each other are now compatible. They fit together. 2 Corinthians 5:18 says, "All of this is from God who reconciled [*what's the next word?*]…**us!**" Who got reconciled? Us. To whom? God Himself.

The new locks had to be changed to the old key. The opposite of that was not an option. It was completely an unworkable option to try to change the old key to fit the old and new locks. God wants a relationship with you so much that He desires to reconcile you. God, like the key, is not going to change. In order for the two of you to fit, God has to change you.

In order for you to fit with God, God will not begin pulling a stinky wagon of His own. No! He will empty yours. It is not a matter of changing your behavior. Your behavior is so inconsistent

> God wants a relationship with you so much that He desires to reconcile you. God, like the key, is not going to change. In order for the two of you to fit, God has to change you.

it's like the weather. If being reconciled to God were a matter of your behavior, you would be reconciled, then the next day un-reconciled, then reconciled, un-reconciled on the weekend, and on and on. You'd be praying to God to make sure you would die on one of the good days!

One of two things must happen for us to be reconciled with God: either God must change, or we must change. And we've already established that God's not changing. What's in our little red wagon becomes a barrier between us and God. God is like fire, and we're like paper. Paper and fire are not reconcilable. We are unholy and unrighteous, and God is holy and righteous. If God isn't going to change His nature, then something has to change in us.

We must be made to fit with Christ permanently so that there is no longer any conflict between God and us, and the contents of the wagon are a non-issue.

2 Corinthians 5:19 says, "God was reconciling the world to Himself in Christ, not counting men's sins against them." What does it mean that God was not *counting?* The word *counting* here is an accounting term, meaning "to calculate." God no longer calculated sin into the relationship. He no longer applied sin to their account. The bottom line is that what God accomplished on the cross makes it possible for sin to no longer be a factor in the equation. He can empty a wagon as though there was never anything in it to condemn you. He can reconcile you and fix you so that sin never has to be discussed again in terms of the relationship.

Now pay attention! When you are reconciled to God, the contents of your wagon can never again sever the connection between you and Him. He will no longer credit the sins to your account. You will fit together. His system is not just for the moment of your salvation as if, now that you know better, you are responsible to handle your own sins. In other words, you enter a relationship with God through grace and you live in a relationship with God through grace. In reconciling He is not counting men's sins against them. He is counting them against Jesus. The junk in your wagon—what you did, what you are doing,

> **When you are reconciled to God, the contents of your wagon can never again sever the connection between you and Him.**

what you intend to do—will have been counted to Christ, and nothing will ever get between your relationship with God again.

God knew that we could not accomplish what it would take to make Him okay with sin. He sent Jesus to take care of that.

chapter 5 questions:

What is the benefit of God never changing?

What is the difficulty in believing that because of Jesus God is willing to never hold your mistakes against you?

Why is it so important to us to be able to do something that earns God's forgiveness and love?

let go of the wagon

My friend, Sam, recently put his faith in Christ. He wasn't looking for God. Like the prodigal son, he lived his life the way he wanted and was involved in some very serious sin. Had his salvation required him to exchange something of value with God, he would have been out of luck. He had nothing to bring to the table. In a nutshell, Sam's little red wagon smelled like rotten fish.

Sam encountered God one day, and all he could say was, "God, You are going to have to accept me as I am. I have nothing to offer.

You must do all the reconciling. I'm absolutely bankrupt when it comes to righteousness."

No exchange of goods or services took place between Sam and God the day he came to Christ. Sam had nothing to offer of equal value to exchange for his salvation. Salvation, or freedom from his red wagon, was God's gift to him.

2 Corinthians 5:17 says, "Therefore if anyone is in Christ he is a new creation, the old has gone, the new has come." To be "in Christ" means you are a Christian. This passage describes what happens to us when we choose to put our faith in Jesus.

This verse doesn't refer to anything that we "do" to earn salvation. The verse describes something that only God can do.

God says that you are a new creation. When you become a Christian, a fundamental change occurs at the level of your spirit, completely aside from your own effort or influence. God makes you new. He is the only "doer" in the salvation process.

God makes you new. He is the only "doer" in the salvation process.

This newness does not always manifest itself immediately in changed behavior or beliefs. But there is a fundamental change that happens. You can discern it, but you can't define it or put your finger on it. You know it's there, but you may not know what "it" is. The Bible says that you are a new creation. God is the One who does this work.

2 Corinthians 5:18 tells us plainly, "All of this is from God who reconciled us to Himself through Christ." There is no role for you to play in the process.

Certainly there are other verses in the Bible that talk about our doing this or that, but when it comes to what God is talking about you don't get to play. This is not an all-skate; you just sit and watch. This passage teaches us that when we become Christians, God fundamentally changes us at the core of our beings. We become somebody we were not before, and this is something God does all by Himself. Quit believing that what is in your wagon is a legitimate excuse to stiff arm God and not receive His free gift of salvation.

chapter 6 questions:

What do you have to offer God?

What would it mean to you if the "old" could be removed from your life and you could be made "new"?

Is there an obstacle in your life today, a wall, that you sense stands between you and a relationship with God?

chapter 7

wave goodbye to your wagon

Like the prodigal son, we can feel distant from God. So we look for a way— any way—to close the gap. Sometimes we try to pay for our mistakes with promises and confessions, and we do a lot of good works to try and gain God's favor.

I talk to people often who suffer all kinds of consequences because of sin: broken relationships, estrangement from their kids, debt, addiction; the list goes on and on. They have all kinds of things they're dealing with, and they tend to see these things as barriers that stand between them and God. When life is hard, we feel that we are being punished and being judged. We feel very much ashamed and sepa-rated from God. We figure that God is against us because of our circumstances.

The good news is that when you come to God, He opens His arms and receives you with no questions asked. No matter where you are or what you've done, you can receive His mercy.

> **The good news is that when you come to God, He opens His arms and receives you with no questions asked.**

55

You show up with your wagon full of good decisions or bad mistakes, and no matter the size of your sin, God is bigger. His arms are wider; His love has more depth, and His grace is stronger. When you ask God to forgive you, and you give your life to Him, nothing can ever again separate you from His love and acceptance. You don't have to empty your wagon or get cleaned up first, but you do have to receive His gift of salvation.

As I sit here and write this chapter, it is my sincere prayer that you would come to a place where you do just that. The Bible indicates that the reason Jesus came was to seek and to save those who are lost. I would have no greater privilege than to pause right now and ask you if you are ready to receive the free gift of salvation.

If you are ready and willing, would you take a moment and pray in your own words something like...

Dear God,

I know I am a sinner and that I have messed things up, but right now I ask You to come into my life to be my Lord (you call the shots in my life), my Savior, my Forgiver, and my best friend. In the best way that I know how, I want to turn my life over to You, and I turn my back on my sin and my self-effort. I trust You alone to be my Savior.

Thank you, Jesus, for saving me!

If you prayed that prayer and meant it with all of your heart, the Bible indicates that Jesus just stepped into your life. This was the smartest decision you have ever made! Congratulations!

chapter 7 questions:

What is the best gift any one has ever given you?

Do you find it easy or difficult to accept something for free? Why?

Can you think of a time when you felt like God was against you because of your circumstances in life?

What are some things you have felt like you should clean up before you come to God?

chapter 8

i am new

When you put your faith in God and you completely trust Him, everything changes because everything is settled. So, let go.

Understanding and believing your mistakes and the fact that the junk in your wagon no longer counts against you empowers you to release your grip. It frees you from pulling the weight of the good and the bad you have done. You no longer have to measure yourself by your accomplishments or even the last time you talked to God…because now…you are a part of

Him. You are free because you are new, because you are now in Christ, and you are held by Him.

Of course, as the renovation of your life continues, you will be tempted from time to time to reach for the handle of your red wagon, but don't do it. Putting your faith in performance and attempting to earn God's favor is useless. The reality of putting your faith in God is that you are transformed, and you are no longer reliant on what you do, but on what Jesus did.

We have to remember that throughout God's story, good deeds always end up falling short of His standard! Why? His standard is too high. Every time you try to measure your goodness against God's benchmark, it is always a net loss. Not even Billy Graham or Mother Teresa perfectly reflect God's goodness—even they lose the comparison game. Why? Because God is perfect. He is holy and righteous, and there is *none* that can equal Him.

Only one man ever measured up to God's standard: Jesus. So God took Jesus, the only One who consistently got it right, the only One who could come to God based on His own deeds and goodness, the only One who was perfect—and placed on Him all of our sin. He became all of the junk in our wagons. Look at 2 Corinthians 5:20-21:

> "For God made Christ, who never sinned, to be the offering for our sin, to become sin itself."

Picture that! The perfect Son of God became what is unacceptable in your wagon so that you might become acceptable to God. By Jesus becoming something

He fundamentally was not, our nature was exchanged for Jesus' nature, and so we are now…new. The result of accepting Christ as your Savior, of placing your complete faith in Him, is your own personal internal transformation as Jesus' nature is now your nature. You fit with God as perfectly as Jesus fits. You are reconciled.

Verse 21 finishes, "…so that in Him we might become the righteousness of God." When you are in Christ, you become the righteousness of God. You are made as righteous as Jesus Himself.

Maybe you are thinking, *There is no way God sees me like*

> When you are in Christ, you become the righteousness of God. You are made as righteous as Jesus Himself.

Jesus. I can't be as righteous as Jesus. Obliterate that thought. Because if you are not as righteous as Jesus, you are incompatible with God, and you don't truly accept what Jesus did for you on the Cross. Jesus died to give you His nature, to ensure your compatibility with God.

God changed you so that you now fit with Him and have been reconciled to Him. The only way to do that was for Him to give you the righteousness of Jesus as a free gift, not because of anything good in your wagon. And get this: your righteous standing can't be taken away because of anything you've done wrong. Who made you righteous? God did. So leave your wagon outside—it is completely irrelevant. What you have done, right or wrong, no longer factors into the relationship.

chapter 8 questions:

What has Jesus done that makes it possible for you to let go of your wagon?

If God sees you through Jesus, what does He see?

What does it mean to you to know that it is not about what you are or what you have done, but it's all about what Jesus did for you on the cross?

chapter 9

me...like Christ?

In coming to God for salvation, we've taken the first step and the only step we are required to take from that point on. God wants us with Him! He created us! He wants to be with us. In His desire to redeem the world, He offered His own Son as a sacrifice. In salvation we become a reflection of Christ, the blameless One.

When we first come to God, most of us come because we need Him to fix our messes. God's solution is to make us like Christ. But is that what we wanted? What we bargained for? What we sought? To be like Jesus?

When I came to Jesus, I just wanted to be a better Alex. Truly! I had no notion of becoming just like Jesus. I mean, what a steep hill to climb! (Too big a hill, for sure, for my abilities.) So my thought was, *Yes, God, come in and fix all my bad stuff. But what I think is good—leave that alone!*

After God gets us in line and back on our feet, often with more favorable natural consequences because of our improving thoughts and actions, we often thank Him and then show Him the door! "Thanks for coming," we say, but what we really mean is, "I'm fine now. Really! You've been just terrific, but You can go now. I can handle the rest by myself." Honestly, what I really wanted when I asked God to come in, was to come out of the experience a better me, a better Alex, an improvement over what I already had going. At that point I really had no idea of what God's blueprint for me was or what He wanted me to look like.

Have you ever looked at a blueprint? There are lines indicating windows and doors, and lines showing stairs. There are different floor plans for different levels of the building, circles for air vents and sinks. For a few individuals, a blueprint can come alive in his or her head, and the person can visualize the building as it will look in three dimensions. It's a gift some have. But for most of us, we want to see a smaller scale, 3-D replica of the structure with a removable roof and little models of our furniture so we can see if this is the home for us. Or we visit a "model home" and walk through, deciding whether we want the staircase near the front door or whether we want two closets instead of one.

The Old Testament law is more like God's blueprint for His people. He showed us what we were designed to be like as His image-bearer. When you read Deuteronomy, surely there are a lot of "to do" or "not to do" lists, but there is also a lot of explanation for why the law is written a specific way.

To many of us these laws are much like the mysterious lines on a blueprint; they can be hard to interpret lying there flat on the pages of our Bible. So God sent Jesus to walk the earth and live among us so we'd have a 3-D representation of what He wants us to look like as we walk, talk, and interact with others.

When you ask God what He wants your character to look like, He will point to a person, His incarnate Son Jesus, not to a list. In the Bible God is saying very plainly, from Genesis through Revelation, "I want you to look like My Son, to love like Him, to be patient like Him, to have self-control like Him. This is the model; go for it."

At this point we often get overwhelmed and resign or give up. We might be able to fine-tune our *own* character, but *be like Jesus*?! We conclude, "There is no way! Jesus is an unattainable model."

Sometimes when faced with this extraordinary new model for our lives, we just give up. We insist, "I am what I am and just about as good as I'm ever gonna get," and we ask everyone around us to accept us the way we are. But, have you ever noticed how rarely we accept this attitude in others? How many of you would accept your two-year-old saying, "I'm just a food-thrower. It's the way I am, and you must accept me."

Would you keep a friend who says, "I'm just a thief; accept me." Would you be happy with a spouse who says, "I am just a spender. Make more money. I cannot change." We don't accept others playing Russian roulette with *our* lives, yet we draw a little circle around ourselves and ask that others love us just the way we are should we decide to play a deadly game with our own lives.

At the core of this attitude is the desire to be accepted without preconditions. The good news begins with the fact that God does accept you just as you are. God's love and acceptance is not luke-warm. God doesn't just tolerate you; He celebrates you! He loves you so much that

> God's love and acceptance is not lukewarm. God doesn't just tolerate you; He celebrates you!

71

He sacrificed His own Son to establish a relationship with you. And the good news continues: God will be doing whatever work it takes to make you an image-bearer of Jesus. He knows you can't do it, and His plan is to be sure your transformation is complete.

In the spring of my sophomore year in college, a church in Pine Bluff, Arkansas, came to the ministry department to hold interviews for a youth intern position for the upcoming summer. I was offered the position in April and was asked to report for service on June 1. During the intervening period, the youth pastor that I was supposed to work under left to work for a different church. When I arrived, the Pine Bluff church decided to hire me as *the* replacement to the youth pastor—not just as an intern. In what seemed like a heartbeat, I was introduced to church politics, called on to speak every week (which was horrifying to me after some simply awful earlier speaking experiences), and required to lead a youth group while I was little more than a youth myself. Feeling overwhelmed and woefully underprepared, I cried myself to sleep many nights in the small parsonage provided for me near the church. One night I found myself sitting on the edge of the old antique bed staring into the mirror across the room in tears. I told God, "I quit." And I'll never forget God's response, "Good."

I was expecting some kind of motivational speech—a kick in the behind, a brilliant ministry concept—something to help me keep going. I was expecting anything but, "Good!"

I repeated, "No, God! You didn't hear me! I said, I quit!"

Understand (as He did) that I was telling Him that I wasn't ready just to quit youth ministry; I was ready to quit all of Christianity. Forever!

But God simply repeated, "Good. Good, Alex. You are right, you can't do it. There is only One who can live the Christian life, and you are not that person. The only One who can live the Christian life is My Son, Jesus".

That encounter I had with God at an early age and stage in ministry has shaped much of the ministry that God has given me. Freedom comes with the realization that the ministry that God calls me to is the ministry that He (and only He) will do in and through me.

Paul tells us in Phillipians to work out our salvation. He did not tell us to work for or earn our salvation; his instruction is to work it out. I think what he is trying to help us understand is that our salvation is complete on the inside, and that we are to work that "out" into our lives. Looking like Jesus is something that Jesus and only Jesus does on the inside of us when we invite Him in. He alone is capable of this. We are to allow what is done on the inside of us to work its way into our thoughts, our actions, and our attitudes.

chapter 9 questions:

What is drawing you into a relationship with God?

What is it about Jesus being the model for your life that seems unattainable?

What is God waiting for you to give over to Him?

chapter 10

don't confuse righteousness with religion

Ok, so here's what we know: at the moment we begin a relationship with Jesus Christ, we are made righteous. We didn't do anything to earn it, and we can't do anything to keep it. In coming to Christ, we are MADE righteous. But what does that really mean? Many of us have the Webster idea of righteousness in our minds. Webster defines *righteousness* as "acting in accord with divine law," or simply "moral." Oh, so to be righteous, I must remain "moral", you ask? Nope. See, God's idea of righteousness is simply to have faith in Him. In the Bible righteousness refers to a relationship between God and us. In Romans Paul explains that Abraham was "declared righteous" because of his faith in God. The Message version calls that "being fit before God." Romans 4:23-24 tells us, "this declaration of righteousness was not for Abraham alone, but also for us who believe in Him." Righteousness is simply added to our account by God because of our faith in Jesus.

When we give our lives to Jesus, we change our system of beliefs, and as a result, our lives begin to change. It's like we look at life through a different lens. Our thoughts, actions, behaviors, and choices all begin to change. We start treating people differently. We stop lying [as much]. We start making better choices [most of the time]. Note the parentheses. We don't suddenly become perfect; we are just drawn to act differently. As Christians, the Holy Spirit now guides in truth and convicts us when we are not acting like followers—like it or not.

Let me caution you here! The temptation after you become a Christian and get plugged into a church is to drift towards religion. Resist it! No amount of Bible study, prayers, church attendance, or hours of service will ever make you more righteous, regardless of what the church may teach. Don't misunderstand me. These are all good things and are essential for spiritual growth, but done out of obligation, they become filth in our wagon.

Making a better you has never been
God's goal. His goal is to make you Christ-
like, and the character of Christ is not
something that you or I can manufacture.
The character of Christ does not come
from piling endless "good things" into your
wagon. It is something God produces in
you. My encouragement to you, as it was
with my friend Sam, is to walk in grace. This
is to remember that it will never be about
what we do, but about what Jesus did.

Righteousness can be tricky. Not "it,"
but rather what "it" does to us. The
moment our relationship with Christ
begins, it's as if our wagon and all of its
contents are emptied and our wagon is
perfectly clean. Like new. At the moment of
salvation, we should simply let go of the
wagon and walk away in freedom, but
here's where the trickiness comes in. The

temptation, again, is for us to pick the handle back up and begin walking proudly with our shiny, newly cleaned wagon for the whole world to see. As our lives begin to change, and our behaviors begin to look more like Jesus, we begin to consider our righteous actions as the essence of what makes us righteous. We understandably become proud. After all, we've carried around and piled on our filthy, disgusting sinful actions for so long it feels good to act right for a change. Naturally, we begin to feel like, "I must really be making God proud, and He must really love me now." We forget that it began with God loving us when we were filthy, and He will never love us more or less. Our righteousness is in spite of us, never because of us.

Remember, the older "good boy" brother in the parable of the prodigal son?

In that story the older son ended up not going into the party with the father. When the father asked him why he would not come into the party, he answered, "Because *I* have always served you." When righteousness is ours instead of God's, it is as repulsive as the sin that used to be in our wagons.

I once sat down to compile what I called, "New Testament Law." There are a lot of rules in the New Testament, a lot of things that Peter and Paul commanded us to do. *Surely*, I thought, *this would be a useful list, so I could know without question exactly how best to please God with my behavior.* Have you ever wondered this? The first book of the New Testament did two things to my quest: It answered my question, and it made a mockery of my foolish quest to discover all New Testament law.

In Jesus' sermon early on in the book of Matthew, He commanded, "Be **perfect**, therefore, as your heavenly Father is perfect" (5:48). And in Matthew 19:21, He says to a rich young man, "If you want to be perfect, go, sell your possessions and give to the poor, and you will have treasure in heaven. Then come, follow me" (19:21). *Be perfect like God? Sell everything I have?* Jesus convinced me quickly that I wouldn't find such a compilation of "New Testament Law" to be inspiring. I felt completely discouraged!

You see, my quest would have confused the essential message given by the New Testament. Jesus did not summarize the law as, "Be perfect." Jesus summarized the law in Matthew 22:37-40: "Love the Lord your God with all your heart and with all your soul and with all your mind. This is the first and greatest commandment."

> It's liberating to have a relationship with someone who loves you no matter what.

The question that begs here is *why?* Why and/or how can righteousness be so confusing? This confusion, I think, may come about because the church still blurs the line between relationship and religion. "Religion" is about following rules and acting right and looking good. Religion unintentionally promotes the "wagon syndrome." It provokes you to pick up the wagon and make sure you have more good than bad in it. An intimate relationship, however, with a God who loves lavishly, forgives endlessly, and provides graciously is the antithesis of religion. It's liberating to have a relationship with someone who loves you no matter what. You can follow the Bible's teachings and attend church for a very long time believing that you are following God because you love Him, but still be filling your wagon with filth all over again. When it becomes about what *you* do, your righteousness becomes self-righteousness. Sin.

Self-righteousness was strongly condemned by Jesus. His harshest criticism was reserved for the Pharisees. These were a well-behaved, well-meaning religious group of people who thought that loving God meant strictly following hundreds of strict rules. See, it can be very hard to give up what you believe is good and pleasing to God and accept that there is nothing you can do to be right with Him. However, once you start to experience the gifts of God, instead of measuring some presumed consequence or value, you'll want to stop pulling around any wagon at all so that you can simply dance in Christ. You'll want to celebrate.

The other great challenge to being in relationship rather than religion is culture. The American culture demands that we be successful. Think about it. From Avis's slogan, "we try harder," to the phrase, "if at first you don't succeed, try and try again", we live in a culture that values self-sufficiency. In fact, our culture honors it. This begins with our parents applauding our first steps, and from that point on, we are conditioned to seek approval and acceptance by what we do. So it stands to reason that when it comes to entering a relationship with God, we simply find it hard to believe that God wants nothing from us. We desire to be successful in our spiritual life, but we mistakenly assume that it comes by hard work. Success may come by hard work in the business world, but not in the spiritual world. In the business world it is about production. In Christianity it's about the person of Jesus.

See, the underlying foundation of all religion is performance. God isn't impressed by our performance. Hebrews 11:6 tells us that faith is the only thing that impresses God. The essence of religion is man's attempt to somehow gain God's approval. It's the way we try to validate our own self-worth, but our acts of self-righteousness actually separate us from the very goal we seek to achieve.

Religion is poison because it kills the opportunity one has to experience genuine intimacy with God.

Religion is poison because it kills the opportunity one has to experience genuine intimacy with God. Religion is what rushes in to fill the vacuum created by the absence of personal intimacy with God.

The person who is trying to achieve spiritual success by religious performance may be making good time, but he or she is driving in circles like the Israelites did for forty years. Trusting in ourselves is not only the default in our culture, but also is applauded by our culture. And God could not disagree more. What we must do is become like little children. God finds a weak or humble person irresistible:

Isaiah 66:2—I will look to the one who is humble and contrite.

Psalm 34:18— The Lord saves those who are crushed in spirit.

James 4:6—He opposes the strong, but those who have been humbled receive grace.

I Cor 1:26-29—We must become weak.

God is glorified in our weakness. He is most pleased with us when we give Him our whole lives. He will live through us when we give up on our own self-efforts and learn to abide in Him. What a beautiful paradox!

So, what are we to do?

chapter 10 questions:

What is the difference between "righteousness" and "self-righteousness"?

What do you do in your life to validate your worth to God?

Look into your own life. Where do you need to become weak?

chapter 11

shiny and new

As we turned down the last aisle, in the eighth antique store we had visited that day, it caught my eye, just off to my right. It was old, but it was in pristine condition. Shiny red with a coal black metal handle, the wagon sat about six inches off the old wood floor on hard rubber wheels with bright white sidewalls. I told my wife, "This is the same wagon I had," and with a nod, she moved on to the next aisle. I just stood there, my mind flooded with the memory of that old red, rusty wagon full of those smelly fish.

Somebody had really taken some time with this antique. They had gone over the old metal frame and sanded away every rusted, rough spot and replaced every bolt and nut. The craftsman had taken what had been worn out and ugly, and with a final coat of paint, turned it into something completely brand new. It had been renewed.

Whether or not we are aware of it at any given time, God is making us new every day in many ways.

Sometimes you see all sorts of flaws in your life, things you shouldn't do and problems that you have. And sometimes, you find yourself learning new things, grasping new concepts, trying new habits and behaviors.

Both are elements of renewal. Sometimes we are taking off old things, and sometimes we are putting on new things. Whether or not we are aware of it at any given time, God is making us new every day in many ways.

The traditional idea of self-improvement involves placing your weaknesses in a pile and devising a system to work on them. While that may make a better you, God's plan is different.

Romans 12:2 says, "Don't copy the behavior and customs of this world, but let God transform you into a new person by changing the way you think."

God has not adopted us and designed us for the purpose of becoming a better person. Making a better you has never been God's goal. His goal is to make you Christ-like, and the character of Christ is not something that you or I can manufacture. The character of

Christ does not come from piling endless "good things" into your wagon. It is something God produces in you. As I mentioned in chapter eight, God is about transformation. How? By renewing our minds. When we renew our thinking, we replace old ways of thinking and take on new ones. God doesn't tell us to rededicate our will, to strengthen our resolve, or to make a new commitment. He tells us that we can be transformed by a new way of thinking.

Look at this verse, "And now, dear brothers and sisters, one final thing. Fix your thoughts on what is true, and honorable, and right, and pure, and lovely, and admirable. Think about things that are excellent and worthy of praise," Philippians 4:8-9.

God doesn't send us down the road with twelve more things to do because He knows we just don't do well in that kind of system. Sure, we can do some good things, but there are temptations that will take us down every time. That's why God wants to transform us, and that begins by renewing our minds. Renewal is the removal of the old and the applying of the new. This is exactly what happens when you strip a piece of old wood furniture and stain it. Years ago we were given an old antique brass bed. We attempted to polish it in the garage for weeks. The process did not work. Remember the frustration I demonstrated with my children? That was nothing compared to the conversations Meredith and I had while attempting to restore that bed. A neighbor informed me that there was a sealer on the brass that would not allow the metal to be cleaned or polished. We had to remove the sealer first, and then we were able to clean and polish the bed.

The renewal of the mind is similar to this process. God takes away our old way of thinking and replaces it with His thoughts or His way of thinking.

Renewal breaks down the resistance to God's will in our lives by giving Him influence and control over our own desires. We see this played out in our relationships with others. When I was first married, I was glad to wash the cars—if it was my idea. If my wife suggested I wash the cars, a little resistance would rise up inside of me.

If I feel this way with the love of my life, you can well imagine and relate to the resistance I sometimes feel toward God directing my life. In my natural state, just like so many of you, I resist the will of God. But as my mind is renewed, my resistance breaks down and I become more receptive to God and to how He wants to work in me.

My second child, Elijah, did not sleep completely through the night even once until he was over two years old. My thought at the time was that my wife, Meredith, was to blame. She babied him far more than she did our daughter, who was almost two when Eli was born. Now, I know better than to say, "Meredith, that was your fault." Eli simply had a hard time sleeping and would cry every night in the middle of the night. Many times I would lose my temper, in frustration, walking down the hall to rock him back to sleep.

One night when he was almost two, I remember rocking him in the glider and having a conversation with God. I remember feeling the Lord say to me, "Alex, you have good friends who would do anything to have a child to get up and rock." What

97

does a renewed mind look like? My attitude changed completely with those renewed thoughts.

Not a thing changed at my house that night except for the renewal of my mind. My thinking changed, but please notice: my thinking didn't change by my own will. I did not decide, *Oh, I need to have a better attitude.* My own will can make me a better Alex, but if I am going to be like Jesus, I need God to change my thinking.

chapter 11 questions:

Why is "renewing the mind" key to transformation?

What are you attempting to fix in your own life right now that is leaving you frustrated and worn out?

How would turning over your frustration and situation to God make a difference?

chapter 12

stay close

Jesus told his disciples, "I am the vine; you are the branches. Those who abide in me, and I in them, will produce much fruit. For apart from me you can do nothing" (John 15:5).

Imagine, for a moment, that you are a branch on a grape vine, and your job is to grow some grapes. As a branch, how are you going to do that? Branches are not designed to receive marching orders, go off, and accomplish a task. Branches produce fruit only because they are attached to the vine.

God has a plan and a purpose for you, but He sees you as a branch, not an agent. You are incapable of producing the fruit that He wants to see in your life. You do not manufacture it; it is produced through you because you are attached to the vine. When you abide with God, you will see patience and self-control and kindness crop up in your life, and you will think, "I am not capable of doing that." In truth, you do not accomplish the remarkable goodness that God works in you—He accomplishes it through you.

The popular slogan, "What would Jesus do?" prompts us to consider Jesus' actions in a given situation. That's fine, if it helps retrain our thinking, but it doesn't make us want to imitate Jesus. For example, what if I want my golf game to improve, and so I decide to imitate a professional golfer. That's laughable. I am completely incapable of imitating any professional golfer or athlete no matter how hard I try. Trust me. So, how can I imitate Jesus?

John 15:4 says, "For a branch cannot produce fruit if it is severed from the vine, and you cannot be fruitful apart from me." What is it, according to this scripture, that will make you unproductive? It is simply being apart from God. If you do not stick close to Him, you will not bear fruit.

Abide is a common Greek word meaning "to remain, to stay, or to move in with, to live with." It is totally a relational word. Roughly translated to modern language, it might read "stay close." That is all…stay close.

If you're like me, you have huge flaws and gaps in your character. I'll fall into a situation and think, *Ouch, I never want to do that again.* But I do, over and over again! I can't seem to reach the point where I never stumble.

Jesus assures me that I don't have to strive for that anymore. He will bridge that gap. He doesn't intend to teach me how; He'll do it through me. So now I just focus on staying close, observing, and watching what He does.

All too often, institutionalized religion tells us that there is a god out there somewhere, and I have to find ways to please him in order to have a relationship with Him. But, this just isn't the case. Did you know that the very term *religion* means "return to bondage"? Isn't that sad? Religion, as commonly practiced, is formal and very legalistic, with an image of God in a sweeping robe. This strict version of God is not accessible to me in any way. I've never worn a robe or been in a kingdom where my fate can be determined by an all-powerful judge. *Religion* (the law) is a lame attempt to stack your wagon with enough good things that somehow the bad things will be overlooked.

> **Relationship with God is very different. It's knowing a person. It's being with someone, staying close.**

Relationship with God is very different. It's knowing a person. It's being with someone, staying close. Relationship is learning to communicate, saying what you're really feeling and thinking, and knowing that you're understood. It's learning to understand someone else. A good relationship is never static. It grows from day to day.

It is living and personal, something unique between you and the one you love.

As parents we all realize that we know more than our children. When my boys were younger (four and two), we lived in a house with a tiered backyard. The upper level sloped, while the lower level was flat providing a great place to put the kids' swing set and other toys.

One day in the fall, the boys built up a huge pile of leaves on the lower level, then got on a tricycle together at the top of the incline and headed downhill, picking up speed with every turn of the pedals. As they reached the end of the tier, they went airborne and shot completely over the top of the leaf pile, crashing into the fence.

Now if they had asked me, "Hey, Dad, what do you think of this idea?" before attempting it, I could have told them that it was a dangerous plan—but, of course, they didn't. In the same way, God has a panoramic view of our life and says, "Please try to view your plans from My perspective. You're rolling into a very dangerous situation in your life."

Learning to see things with God's eyes means that we think differently. This new system is far better than following a list of rules and avoiding forbidden actions. This is a 3-D model of Jesus, who lives inside us and wants to discuss our plans with us, before we decide to pile onto our trikes and go barreling down the slope toward certain disaster.

What is the cry of your heart? Are you a wife who can't deal with her husband coming home late one more time? Or are you a man who stares at his computer, closed up in his study late at night, enslaved by pornography? Are you a woman who has been hurt so badly that you can never forgive?

Go ahead. Wave the white flag. Know that you cannot deal with this problem alone, but God can. The plan is not for you to be a better person or for you to be able to handle every problem that crops up in your life. The plan is for you to walk away from your little red wagon and begin your relationship with God. Crawl onto His lap, and let His life, love, and wisdom flow through you.

You can't, but Jesus can.

chapter 12 questions:

If you are feeling "apart from God" right now, what obstacles do you sense are contributing to your situation?

What would hinder you right now from letting that go, reaching out, and taking hold of God, instead?

Coming soon from Alex Himaya

Jesus Hates Religion

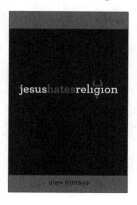

For other resources by Alex Himaya
please check out www.TCABC.com

WORD & SPIRIT
RESOURCES